THIS BOOK BELONGS TO:

THANK YOU FOR YOUR PURCHASE!

We are a small, family run business and appreciate each and every order...

Don't miss out on your freebie

The Take Time to Chill Coloring Collection has 50 awesome digital coloring pages from our different coloring books (and a few bonus pages too...)

To download
- Either scan the QR code here
- Or visit our website:

www.ellastevensondesigns.com

© Copyright 2025 - All rights reserved by EllaStevensonDesigns

Legal notice. This book is only for personal use. The contents of the book may not be reproduced, duplicated or transmitted without direct written permission from the author, except small sections for review purposes.

COLOR TEST PAGE

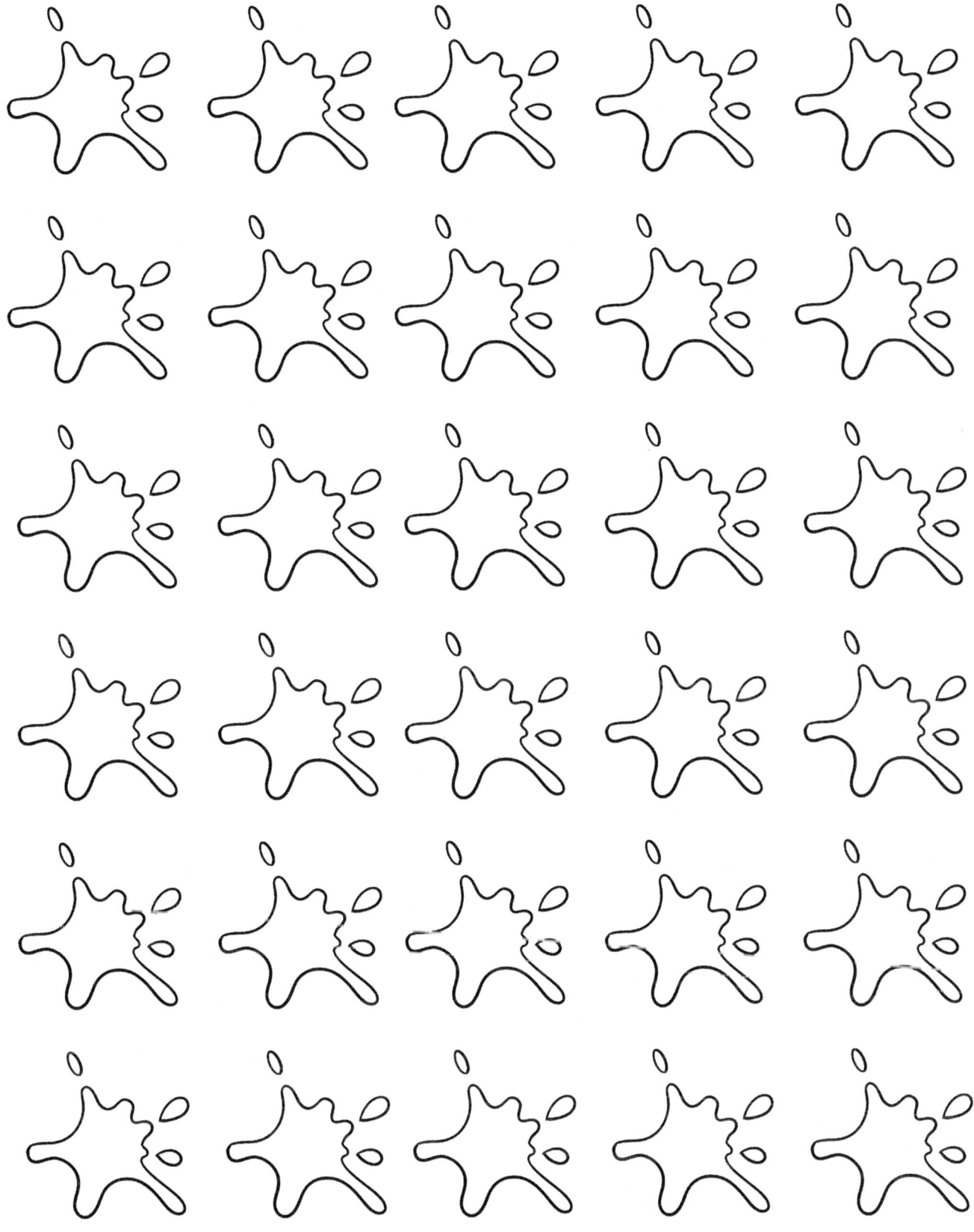

USING FELT TIPS OR MARKERS?

WE RECOMMEND YOU PUT A SHEET OF THICK PAPER OR CARD BEHIND THE PAGE YOU'RE WORKING ON.

IT'S A SIMPLE WAY TO PROTECT THE ARTWORK UNDERNEATH, ENSURING EACH MAJESTIC MARE, SLEEK STALLION OR PLAYFUL PONY REMAINS FRESH AND UNTOUCHED – READY FOR YOU TO BRING TO LIFE.

The paper Amazon uses to print coloring books is best suited for colored pencils and gel pens. If using felt tip pens, we recommend putting a piece of card or paper behind the page you are coloring to prevent any bleed through.

WAIT... THERE'S MORE TO COLOR!

Loved these pages? There are more waiting for you online...

The Take Time to Chill Coloring Collection has 50 awesome digital coloring pages from our different coloring books (and a few bonus pages too...)

To download
- Either scan the QR code here
- Or visit our website:

www.ellastevensondesigns.com

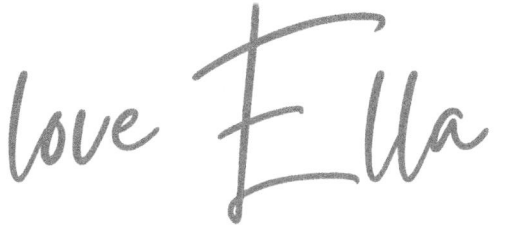

© Copyright 2025 - All rights reserved by EllaStevensonDesigns

Legal notice. This book is only for personal use. The contents of the book may not be reproduced, duplicated or transmitted without direct written permission from the author, except small sections for review purposes.

Printed in Dunstable, United Kingdom